# Broken maps

*Poetry*

## Riak Marial Riak

Mwanaka Media and Publishing Pvt Ltd,
Chitungwiza, Zimbabwe
*
*Creativity, Wisdom, and Beauty*

Publisher: *Mmap*
Mwanaka Media and Publishing Pvt Ltd
24 Svosve Road, Zengeza 1
Chitungwiza, Zimbabwe
mwanaka@yahoo.com
mwanaka13@gmail.com
https://www.mmapublishing.org
www.africanbookscollective.com/publishers/mwanaka-media-and-publishing
https://facebook.com/MwanakaMediaAndPublishing/

Distributed in and outside N. America by African Books Collective
orders@africanbookscollective.com
www.africanbookscollective.com

ISBN: 978-1-77933-148-9
EAN: 9781779331489

© Riak Marial Riak 2024

All rights reserved.
No part of this book may be reproduced or transmitted in any form or by any means, mechanical or electronic, including photocopying and recording, or be stored in any information storage or retrieval system, without written permission from the publisher

DISCLAIMER
All views expressed in this publication are those of the author and do not necessarily reflect the views of *Mmap*.

# Table of Contents

Introduction

After repairing my neighbor's house

No body reaches the height of life

80 days behind trail of light Introduction

The fire in a boy searching for escape route

Boys staring at night sky

The shape of shadow above my eyes

The portrait of a carpenter

The reason why desert is a large mirror in our house

Ali staring at a broken mirror and saw his sister naked

The map showed me I can still leave home

Still a raven will cry

This day

For the boys who examined sun on their feet

The song in my father's eyes

Here is where you can live

The guest is the shadow of a child drawing his body on water

Where faces become hardened by hate

How to love a girl

From The night at Home

Solid grief i drawn on a carpenter's note

Drawing light

How I love to play songs for the war

How to live with bullets

Don't you die son?

At club de havanna when the music went down

On the walls

An epigram of life

For carnage

coming after the wind

The origin of water

The night of those who once where in love

one two and three

Experiment of love where we once fall

The decline of age

Jonathan

Take me to moseluem to touch on statue

Burning city at night

New voices in the rain

The height of moonlight

After the rain drops

Ama

When the light cast on a dim altar

The pathway

Body as a shipwreck for water

The first creation of loss

After midnight song

Boy, how do you live with a joy

One night wiping mud faces

Four girls each sm

Tonight if you sit among the culprits

I hide behind the mirror

Mama Amai

Night later

A little toy city

A sad night to love eliza

Night i crave for your soul

The second rash to kush love

At 11:36 am

More at a constant road

The russet home

(After Alphonso Cikedi)

Antiquity of a night painting

Her question of life

Love or affluence, girl

In our old days

My life

do not sleep child

    Mmap New African Poets Series

# Introduction

To me every individual fights for his/her dignity; it is the battle I believe bring maturity out of mankind regardless of predicaments, torture and appeasement. I think everyone is odd when it comes to trouble and falsehood; it was something copied from generations once inhabiting our earth. I had this belief from childhood until now that all who lives in the world are leaders and fools provided one made it alone.

And here is a Broken map answering the question of our lives, not walking away from difficulties we were born with but is there to mend part of our broken selves. Most of the times the images carry existence and belonging, stories of dedication and conformity will always seek to heal that little breakage left in us by hate, jealousy and discrimination, and all who believes in becoming one once again will revisit the nature of their living, to realize how every mischief could only derail the peace we should have.

Therefore, every poem carries its own soul out of fire, stigma, destitute and despair to live on for ages, words here become alive and for this it has become evident that where ever language tries to flourish Poetry is there for undertakings and this is what Repairing my neighbor's house to each poem following seek to address. Poets speak truth and it is their belief that it's only truth and faithfulness will set mankind free as is the Holy book, how far has man become the ladder to his own downfall, it is always there that one can be the glue to keep closer ties once meant to make people justifiable.

And for little time the mind could be in abeyance dreaming a beautiful dream of success and happiness but art is caught by the fact that anyone living on earth is a warrior and must fight till the end. It is also caught by the fact that anyone living on earth is a student and must learn until the end. These ignominies of the world divided minds and leave it flowing tirelessly; getting untouched things and become inseparable with life afterward, reminding people about challenges that may occur in near future and give it time to understand; it is difficult to intersect this kind of life because many can be separated from the community by the forces of universe

However much the language is a driving force in Poetry, the nature of aesthetics could be felt more and more, making poems digestible. Here is where the beginning correspond to the middle and the end, both metaphorically woven to move gently.

The book opens with a story of man who believes his identity cannot be traced back to his endurance and hostility or through scars on his face but through love and freeness. He wanted to rub love on faces of those walking on that road but it was hard because where he comes suffer deeply from untold tribal rivalries. Other poems follow in the same search for justice which is a hot cake in this part of the world, life of an individual would go unnoticed and whole population wakes with new life.

# After repairing my neighbor's house

      my father comes with sledge hammer
on his shoulder
      i don't know how he keeps whining
but his red t shirt is moistened by value
      of working hard
unless one sweat his life on the back of jacket
      he will never be gentle
this is what i read from first chapter of living
      and many of them say us will call this hustle
that you gripped bones to face life with basking
order
      my father made what is on his shoulder
from particles of gravity
      a force pulling one to be confident
and know how do you want to hold it without blazing
      in the wind
one day i flipped where he started moving on
      and was seen losing aptitude of determination
too many faces ready to relearn how he matches
      thunderstorm on the catalogue of sand
i call this duty, he becomes wet and leave all he was
      doing and soaked his hand into dustbin
too many faces scared to ask my father how
      he became one definition of cleanliness
his hand frothed the follicle of living coming together
one that is bend to symbolize others
      and i flipped till the end never come
my father knows it is life. he knows it will not come

where it does end.

## No body reaches the height of life

for me i have seen wolves
shepherding lambs

and dogs keeping an eye on antelopes
everyone is a friend to the enemy

except the crashes carried down
in the lineage

today a man sits traumatized to know
how to rewind the nature of his life

maybe he will take it to childhood
where everything is a dream

life fought me hard
and i do not want to refuse its fallout

i want to know the height
to measure how it emancipate

and tighten the rip i had with him
every day we reached the bridge

each one seems to make crossing
on his own

i envy how love for life made me blind
i come to know at last that struggle

may mean living in its definition
but at times like this it is light

that flies, the relevant in pure existence
when everything only wanted to fade.

## 80 days behind trail of light

and i said
to those holding lights behind me
move on
the world is not owned

someday i come like the wind
on your hair
and leave
home
more embedded on your lips

and you cannot justify how a hibiscus
opens to vows of sun
and you cannot be conceivable
through stories only read under your footprints

later that night
there's light paving ways into myself
someone doesn't want to walk there
here is what they said

boy you're fortunate that our lamps
can burn in the wind
you shall see the shore

how can you fight bondage fitting into your eyes

every line on this map
is a way back home

i want to rest before birds sing songs
made for scatter
it's our world hiding behind fading lights

and under my feet
is a story of refuge
it is lasting on our faces
move on
for the world may seek to keep
you in flashes
even when it is caged in travail.

# The fire in a boy searching for escape route

and he knelt to savour
fire not seen from his eyes

two men walked into the end
of rivers to learn origin of water

and they ended up dipping
feet into vastness of the meadow

one of them is afraid how darkness
may live in their eyes forever

another one learn stories of shepherd
who hide fears in their smile

the river is a body looking to wake
from sand wiped by wind

he says
his body a way followed by tributaries
sole marshes outgrown its bank

and know every destiny must be met
with dwindling of lights, every day
the sun seek to rest and does not find home

unless it will return into the river
everything made out of fire must be clean

in his eyes there's fire ready to escape
bodies not willing to fight

unless the wind reconsider how it should
ferry them to a good shore
and take them where life is optimal.

# Boys staring at night sky

two boys sat beside the road
waiting for their father to teach
them how stars do not burn
from lashes of sun

at night they become broader
stepping onto pavements
darkness is not seen leaving

every day the sound over radio
is a news of people made to swallow
their history as misfortune

and walked back home to touch
the statue of their origin
some who came this far to know
existence may mean to slaughter
waddled on road of refuge

two boys one of them sat
to count his fingers as many as stars
and at the end move home
to teach his father how people
who left home know every line on the maps

the bigger ones disappearing into sea

unless some that looks tiny
can be rivers, one of them is the nile
and he knows this is where his origin onset

and the other boy who believes
it is only lust keeping him away
he will teach his father how survival
hide under water

there are boys who dived deep to fondle
all the scales that sank longtime ago
some were kept by history
unless those which left home for good sun
will return to bemoan depression
painted on faces of their community

one of them will draw the line coming
into his body
and leave
one of them will follow this line
until it disappears into nile

and many will say
his father made this light out of his bone
he will survive the eroding history

at night the boys stared in the sky
and saw their father sending rain
of light
wiping their eyes to see clearly lines
that will keep them safe
even when some of them look broken.

# The shape of shadow above my eyes

and i buried my eyes
in the swiftness of solitude

today when my grandmother sings
of people not asking for forgiveness

is a story of boys leaving home to harbour
light on their fingers

everyone at the end of life
becomes zig zag after all kissed

what stood in the midst of solicitation
this is how a fly does not want to feel

bounces in the air
except when lights lost into the shadows

one of them will still rise
to look for ways that do not go astray

everyday the sound of wind is annoying
to pass without hearing life leaving into vastness of perches

into restoration, it is today at home i sat disposed
of where to pour my love for yawning

leaves, there may be the question not skipped
when inappropriately asked

every day i asked myself why is grief not the first
thing to disembark out of me

maybe we all can dodge it
and chose to believe in what makes us happy

sometimes it is light seen sneaking out of me
it can be seen with pain in the eyes, on all parts

that can reconstruct life under my feet
the lines banishing after living become inseparable with anxiety.

# The portrait of a carpenter

and every day the sound of footsteps
are coming through my door

in the house where i come to learn
how history made us live with bullets

is a boy calling upon his body
to leave
to find place that repair his bone

and relax when it's not early to escape life
someday the moon will not refuse to walk
into a forest barren of baobab leaves

but it will refuse to walk into our palms
to stumble when everyone repented

at the entrance someone is looking light
in the face
and is fading away, far from how people

keep fire as mean to retrieve living
it is tonight a spider can draw lines

on the walls
conceived after stars broke their vows
to shine as face of the earth

every day is a boy calling for light to divide
his body
other parts that can rise with smoke

and other parts that can carry wound of existence
is why i found all feet burning on wall

in the room when every sound is subsidized
when every shadow feels fading out

unable to be woken by scars that is bend as mirror
to rediscover faces more in need of consternation
and this house is keeping shadows with bodies

wrapped around cobweb of living
and know why a carpenter cannot carry his own cross
at least if his portrait can do

it's all fighting to look light in the face
searching for ways into my door keeping footsteps
to every strange land. the heart of a traveler. sometimes lost in the
wind.

# The reason why desert is a large mirror in our house

a,

the boy searches for stardom on his face for weeks now
he can guarantee his father a legacy
of people who can easily die and resurrect

b,

this is what he was told
for years you searched for where to leave
in your hurt can be tamed
then the road ends with fracas of light
going behind your shadow

c,

you will not come pick the remains
of hair on ways to refugee camp
you will hide light descending on people
craving to be stars

d,

and now are turning back to see how far
their footprints drawn on sand
and know every day one of them is a migrant

rogued to live with blockade on his lips

e,

and inside him a bystander asked for share
of fire in his eyes
nobody knows how to exist without another
except the desert relentless at night
look at how calm it is to find home in your
shadow

f,

there are many who found homes
in setting fire on bodies
a stardom scripted in the mirror, in his eyes
weeping as he wade into water for reservoirs

g,

there's a map where pictures are sheathed
by wind
and they glow after sun reeled on tiny shape
of earth
making each one of them comprehensive
this one like his father carrying history on his face
say, how body is a map to consternation

h,


there's a map cleaved by displacement
a heart can be heavy when it does not see

candles burning from wind soar
now you can die and resurrect
but to him a house stands between water
and fire
one is to swallow you as whole as grain in a windmill
two is to scar your body as oranges in the harmatan
but you can leave searching for stardom
once reinvented in your eyes

today it is at home, in your hurt, in your eyes.

## Ali staring at a broken mirror and saw his sister naked

    (a)

and as he waits for a second
shadow to rise
a smoke first evades every picture
rolling behind pieces of a glass
papa
how can my own sister walked
into me naked
i can feel lust chopping in my belly
and whole lot of pasts consumes
the lower abdomen
to god how can my own sister walked
toward me naked
her body a land between rivers
ordained by light
how holy it is to find this breast
red face and a broken body
once her land harvested milk and honey
she walks toward me nagged
by limbo
a way too far to reach home safe

    (b)
and as i was raving to catch

lean poles
that kept fire surging
another shadow rises
bigger than my eyeballs
this time a picture of two of us
seated around mortar with matches
it can burn our whole bodies, and we can be ashes
and we can rise above sea levels
and formed catalogue of smoke
winking in the face of stars
give me how you desire to leave your body
go with wind
give me where you desire death to befall you
if it is at home, you'll befitting
and if it is above sea levels, then recall turbulence
once rubbed in your face
and that way you walked toward me naked
to demand your last breathe
as if the mirror will consume you tonight
as if death revisit places it once conquered.

# The map showed me I can still leave home

**and a boy sat at the church upfront
waiting for morsel**

to be this mean is not something one hides
his grievances in the eyes

in the book of creation he carves his mother
out of city still yearning for air

he says

how does one leaves his own boundary
to kneel for sun wailing over carcasses of boys

in the end everyone of us heard what his heart says
let's give to him love, let's give to him faith
and we shall be set free

on this map there's home where lines are ways
parched by gunshot

have you seen smoke billowing there
and you become quiet

you wished it's when you're taken behind bars
in that city a boy takes linen clothes
into ways of light, to burn and to be symbolic

where his mother searched for life on his face
and become redundant

on this map he'll draw rivers that flowed into him
and forget how it may return to its origin

can it begin where it does not end
he saw too many roads squeezed by water

and his feet will fall where everyone has taken

and the boy sat waiting for the drawers to show
him maps of exiting
and he may decide not to escape home

some boys who feel safety is becoming silence
have no homes
and will always come to fondle lines on maps
if at all they can exist

his mother said
son don't ever turn deaf ears to men having guns
in their waists
one of them came drunk yesterday

and he might be there to kill the mocking bird.

## Still a raven will cry

papa
how is fire not the last thing to consume
an object desiring moisture

there's a dog yearning to carry moon
on its tail

here a way leading to where it survive, a garden
of milky flowers woken by sunlight

here is a pavement, do you have words on your lips
that explodes like bomb
you will built sanctuary of fire in your eyes

if only are people turning their backs after life
they will walk into paths crooked by too much anxiety

i am running away from this fire
except the candles burning as if to remember how
our faces become partial in escaping darkness

papa to live one must built a house with lights
in his heart
one must beckon stars sifting to mere clouds

this is how life become everlasting on our faces
and we kept it from returning into cages

are we not the same descendants that smashed
river with bare feet

killing marshes to be able to cross when it's slippery

everyday you live
there's a boy fondling moon in his eyes
singing it into song of a dog waving its tail as secondment

papa one day we will sense the future is beyond our love
and if we make it stitched by the lamplight
we will hide our tears and search for belonging

at this time the dogs would be sleeping
and they dreamed of getting fire burning

at this time the dogs would ask to be shown signs
of light rasped on their tails
and say live, papa is a burning candle in the midst of rainfall

that undying fire, it's a desire to grow, to know why a raven still cry.

# This day

i know love is broken
the day mother woke me
to imitate bullets
in the sky of may
in the mirror people chased
after me to know why
i am not devastated by faces
reinvented to carry burden
of their lives
everyday a boy is size of gun
shot in rubkona
a girl is headlines of rape
exaggerating war in the tv
we have come this far
to be how people think
of disgrace
now there are shadows
willing to rest here at home
mother one day a boy
shown me prize of hibiscus
and wanted me buy it more than
the knife
he wanted me buy what world
has soaked in dust
but i know the luster on edges
of this cutlery
it is meant to walk into darkness

and not distort with fear
but how long does flower open
often with smile
this is more assuring to live
to be what people desire as only light
seeping through the window.

# For the boys who examined sun on their feet

and in the courtroom
i promised you
the catalogue of all desires

to kiss you and run away
to seek destiny
in the prattle of guns

how sun is adhesive
to keep one moving?

under the mango tree
two boys share the feathers
of fallen birds
to fly, to return into zest
to wake up chiselling eyes
of a stern light

wherever the feet failed to wade
there's home waiting to receive
you, the whimps, symphonies
of life swayed in the face of sun
and looked down
you will find a promise always
broken

that promise becoming maps
sheathed by belonging

it is at home thousand feet
can find a rest

it is at home a gun
is more precious than candlelight

it keeps one moving into dark
walls

how does a shepherd become holy
without pinching his face
to know life onset with frailties?

here are thousands promises broken
prayed for, disposed
and under their feet home
waits to rekindle anthils of stars

those that  become luscious
after sun tilted like broken palaces
all found crooked, all with bruises
of eroded flower.

## The song in my father's eyes

and the sun can speak
for bodied forgetting they once hold gruntle
midnight i learn songs leaving through
my father's eyes

the reckoning of how man is a remain
of city once filled with air and dance
in his eyes i am trachoma of beats
wilderness can speak

and he was playing his guitar to call home
his own father
in the wall his father said
one man killed a man for allegiance
one man wraps all cities on his body
and is now being sang, folded into map
anyone can find survival

is it not existence, he whined, he stops
the string playing drop drop
and the rain carry voices looking for ways
to belonging

the song in his eyes is sad, say it is a malady
and in his arms i laid to count years
indicted by bloodline in the palms

my father

i have played every song leaving
his eyes
and it is a city where bones are stepping
stone to refugee camps, man do the needful
before erasure, the beats of wildness is becoming
deep and i cannot carry.

# Here is where you can live

on the river bank
we screamed for our brothers
who are swimming far away

tide full of bones
that cannot rise again

in the evening water
come puttering
like bullets over the sky
of our cities
   those where war originated

it is only in the river
one finds arm to cross
   but when the surface
become water bodies

how many will lose their skin
   to the wild creatures of seas

under the deep crawl of sea
   a star fall into water
and not returned

one after the other boys fall into holes
deeper than their bodies

where is that home our ancestors lived
it is said they lived with water

every day a child drowns
every day a government say built dykes
and dams

there are people making their bodies
bridges to live
how many will go to the shore

how long has man become a bird
to fly over the large volume of water

even the birds carry grass as their bridge
when feathers unable to carry on

what can we carry
the bones of our dead relatives, horns
of our magnificent bulls

or leave the sea shatter lights
in our eyes
every day we drown a dyke is said to be built

now anyone willing can built it on our bones
for we are condemned to live
to be how our ancestors existed with this surface
of water.

# The eulogies of living

a death
is lacking fire

a tree is moisture
leaning to breathe
thru its leaves

a living
is both death and tree
last it can have fire
when leaves spring
on stem

anything lacking fire
is coward

anything carrying moisture
and fire is succinct

and death being coward
fight thing made it look
immortal, life

and death being coward
leans into  invisibility

who will bother to fight
a coward

everyone has learned to live
with you

when you lacked fire
we will fuel you with tears

and death being coward
fights life
and it is there when no one needed
him.

# The guest is the shadow of a child drawing his body on water

and he said
how about the child licking water
on his body

how does wind tore his umbilical cord
does he kiss the wind to keep fire on his body

or will he leave to persuade promises
that do not exist

today a child weeps for his mother
smudging feet to see portion of luster

and when it becomes a parapet
life can be at where it desires to leave

even homes smoke rasped on chimneys
today the child opens a padlock

and become key to ways of living
in the air a fly is tired of giving moisture

to bodies burning of stigma
how can it be heavier than weight of envy
in his heart

to swim, to live and to die
this is the day one fly broke its wings

searching for sanity

and in the aftermath of profound craving
it got tired to wade home with nothing

except how to be wild
on a canvas he will draw his face gripped
by fear, that to harbour silence is to let fire

consume roofs that gives light a residence
on a canvas there's little hole where water

flow, that lagoon safe for amphibians
is becoming home for mankind

how bizarre it is to let water bury your bones
when you do not know where to live

on a canvas he looks for his umbilical cord
swallowed by creatures made by their thirst
to exist.

# Where faces become hardened by hate

i. where hate become scorches
of heat in our hearts

   does it mean to plug eyes
to be one people

ii. where faces crooked by guilt
is there sentiment
in riding love for discord

iii. today i sit here flipping pages
of my heart to read last chapter
that Speaks of redeeming self

   to be whoever dogs do not bark
at his movements
     to stroll under auspices of compassion

to give what people think is privacy
      to love who finds his destiny
in following where my feet had not taken

iv. where i live a fly winked at its creator
     rapacious in the grass to rediscover
it's ways of living

   for long we have longed to disembark
     on oneness

here the scorches existed
  and we are deemed to carry
always us who can die from the scars

of disunity. all of us who came this far
  to be nothing

after so much bruises. after so much estrangement.

# How to love a girl

1. you hold her arms folded into misery
and give what belongs to her, give her pens
and a blank paper to write the meaning of her existence
and she will write DREAM

2. you say
Determined
to
Reconsider
Endurance
of
Alleviating
Mother
and in her eyes a life fogged by desire
to hatch men with broken maps
how do you get back to yourself when this bridge
is shattered long time ago

3. in her palms there's light drawn to wipe your scars
and become a boy not turning away from his shadow
she will fondle this map of existence in you
and in the cradle of your heart you will only write LOVE

4. you will say
live
give
and lit the room to find her place
out of gloom
she will always remember this profound
DREAM to be loved

to be looked at when every map is shattered.

# From The night at Home

both. are evolutions of the planet
OPUSCULE
   with taunted lips
a boy shot one of shining lights
   and into mimesis
afraid of walking back to where he belongs
   both. are evolutions of a refugee
camps
leaving into homes plugged
by water streaming from sudd land

   how do i carry your face in my heart
god made me live
   from things between man's teeth
are leaking one after the other
both. are evolutions of children
born to scalped war in their palms
how long the night in your eyes

it is weary and a man plunged his tongue
to nothingness
to everywhere he calls displacement
masses of stars running into clouds
and move at once
   divided rooms and i found myself
hidden on a soft wall
   home

   a diminutive luster
both. are evolutions of war
god how much is a fare to one's self

im always reminded of a distorted images
  are we both. the evolutions of anything
undesirable
    make us upright, make us look steady
in anything desirable
    this tufted gown worn when darkness
surpassed
this light rubbed on our lips
both are evolutions of planet LIVING.

# Solid grief i drawn on a carpenter's note

i

and today as i sit
moon fantasies
on last train carrying us home

juba, clouds of smoke
and where to be safe

i got one kick for saying
praise the quiet man

for being ladder to stifle
he said his voice is lost
blueness of the pavement

ii

on a carpenter's note
he wrote
"carry your own scar"

i am late for tomato paste
one slice and my fingers
dipped in rashness

how do you not live
to find home
in your scars

iii

everyday i enter myself
a boy mistook notes
for bandage of grief

and he will stop the train
and lost into juba
a profound city holding our names

on scale of boundaries
how do you not hide grief
in your broken knees

iv

you are ever there to ferry
us, to be shadow burying
our bodies glued by bruises

how do i weep
when they say my footprint
is a door to existence

on a carpenter's note
i will always drawn ways
to rekindle my scars

ways to get that gazumping

fire
to gape at the train
and fall in love, juba, a cloud of smoke.

# Drawing light on a canvas

baba
you looked into sky
tears made light
on the leaves of pumpkin

how do you not see sky
crooked by camouflage
　how do you not see fire
running on stream of ice flake

on your face a boy kissed
his dead father
　saying Allah Kareem
you died searching for where to trust

how do you not see home
a jungle of bullets
in your eyes a man chase after man
holding knives to stab their backs

a mean to gain freedom
baba
my freedom is a swirling smoke
over towers of wad alfa

it's a gunshot in omdhurman
the problem of Sudan
mashakil ad Sudan

if the water is your body

then may i drink it into my belly
and i will taste flavors of life
it is love, is steeping light

on a canvas
weighing to burn with nimble
of sun
at night i am eager to die for
a boy mistaking his sister for a stranger

he'll say
rape the hell out of her
and in wad medini the bus
is yelling for people whose home
erected in a hollow cemetery

baba
are gods not happy
that you drawn lights from gunshot
on a canvas

they are prattling, they are not quiet
our sudans are crying, our sudans are not quiet.

# How I love to play songs for the war

one of them is Miriam
how sweet is freedom

a poet was shot in the head
for saying
he's divorced silence

for holding the hands of a widow
and walked into city forgetting
how to forgive her people

and when they found bodies
they cannot weep
they fight for every survival

to escape camouflage
rising in their eyes

in one of the apartment
two boys play guitar
after hearing beats on radio

beats that talk of people
devastated by their willingness
to scatter

how about this song
coming through the window
it sings of a fly lost in the snow
trying to recover his way home

how are we not this bird
every day i walked into this city
is to retrieve my feet left here
as a measure of history

on my body i have lost culture
of punishment
how people cut wound on my face
and say my forefathers lived this way

on my body air fades into burning
light
for this long our scares are what we made
everlasting

say
how Miriam died searching for freedom
in her voice

say
how a poet is shot in the head
for divorcing silence

say
the birds lost in the snow looking
to escape its fears.

## How to live with bullets

and here under the acacia tree
i sense a black stone lighted by snowfall
one day at home people think so much
of my lust to grow into a man
one day i looked inside my palms
and air slowly fades into minarets
building bonds unbreakable with pores
when you pray, you will always pray
to be a man
to see things bigger than your eyes
and run after them
this is a way your dad called redemption
to take a gun in middle of night
and examine future out of its trigger
here i have lived with every bullet
shot in 24hours
and who is scared of things put to exist
with us in the beginning
a law maker laugh at how his governor burns
men to ashes
and here the black stone is a bone left
when fire walked on four village men
this is how to exist
 he says
at night you will see dim lights on the street
only when you are ready to hide bullets
in your skin
go on and rest,

# Don't you die son?

don't you die son?

i asked you to know talking
about people that dump bodies
in trenches of jebel mara
can make you lifeless
remember fear is one thing to have your
life
in the room i saw mother praying
for her son that fights with crushes
of future
she says
to live here at home is to be coward
to smile at men taking your elder
brother into bushes
to learn wildness
i will have love your silence
to watch boys shot a woman
for speaking language they do not hear
in the street she gave her only son
to the boys firing bullets on her chest
that day her son thought
this is the way to live
and promise to hide in the barrel of gun
even in his own room
having no faith in candles
burning on his wall

there's a picture of his mother
smiling back at him
there's a picture of a boy wrapped
in sackcloth
and dumped in the pit
that way is how to be safe
from boys leaving with blood on their tongues
home is not peaceful
if to live is to be silence.

# At club de havanna when the music went down

one day we will go back to de havanna
to drink anything that remains
for all
love, life, living and even death
for all of us have seen a guitar
as much as the size of a despicable
gun
and we have nothing to say
we have nothing to beat
with our bare hands
except the pulse of crackling
wall, how it can burn your fingers
and desire rain falling on your hair
on your feet
walk on it, just leave home
for where sound of a gunshot
is as distant as planet Mars
leaving it soothing
as that music on the radio
on the balcony of de havanna
where we always run to exist.

## On the walls

and he walked into walls
looking to find light
that lasts over his body

that cannot diminish
and become past
like how two men carried sun
to the east to rise once again

but now as he sit love rotates
in his heart
and it is said that's how earth
moves around orbit

that's why sun rises and set
and love will also rise and set
on our faces, wherever it is rooted

he will know the weight of his zest
and breathe for others to run after
their shadows
at home, wherever his feet is printed

each one looking into the face of sun
is to carry his burden
each one fragmented into moonlight
is to weigh his living

and not return to war with himself
and not strip himself of faith and luster

each one must search his body for redemption

after he found light shooting into walls
after he found light not owned.

# An epigram of life

and if you stare
at your own shadow
it is life walking
toward you

the harmatan wind
eased into your skin
without difficulty

take the fire
and know about
being grateful

you'll blink in the rain
made murals
in the lapping of lakes

you'll get on with smoke
into deep sky
obssessed of wetness

pray
every guardian keeps
flashes of light on the face
to make himself free,
to be alive.

## For carnage

    out of anger or hunger man alone found
    way to feed his bones to wild birds
    and the cameraman would say
    "film this one well, it will sell globally"
    and they photographed the wildness
    of the scene, thick, dark with raging war
    in his eyes
isn't this easy to chase off vultures
by sparing someone's wrong deeds?

## coming after the wind

a sky vapour
is the cough in my throat

i want to kiss my baby
on the forehead

his skin become crampy
as wind stole itself
into his body

run baby
run from piercing of songs
after wind burst

escape how to die
the wind is an instrument

for measuring weight
of grief

will your tears take you home
will it banish and leave
destiny plow in your sight

escape how to burn
for wind is a force pulling
you to places of thorns

escape how to be kneaded
to stones not displaying
how desire is an everlasting fire

run baby
run before wind plucked
your hair

every downpour is wild, is inexhaustible
is hurts and is broken.

# The origin of water

and the gleaming pools

bubble

bright when its shores woke

frozen by night wind

baba sat at the door

counting nimble rasped in the stars

counting wars layered in the moon

he is misspelling home in his heart

can it be mourn, can it be thorn

last night he went into the garden

to ask his god about forgiveness

and his god soaked body into water

for glamour

one day you walked into light naked

and ye shall returned into it naked

this is what he fought for at the door

this is why he washed his body

dried upon the tide

sun tossed into deep putters of water

and find life as tidy as nymph

wiping its wings in the cradle of stars

this is the origin of water

blessedness, incandescent, flames

and the body became water

and the body became lustrous

god sat looking me in the face

saying jump into the sea

and you'll be safe from the fire

in your eyes.

# The night of those who once where in love

## one two and three



one

and it's 2 33 am
fades life into the wall
and kiss everything living in air

the body is turned to midnight
song
and all tromped in for residue

do not look back
we are all ahead of you
time cannot live without a memory

i know in the night
people will begin to move on
and say this is how love does


two

you do not need a river
how bout your eyes
appalled by compassion

give man what he desires
give him particles of unbent
petals he will hid grimace

in his eyes
the night will not be long
just is lambent a footnote

waddled on a dim screen
you do not need a river
you need a soft heart
to moisten body


three

and it's 2 47 am
i do not know which song
to carry in my heart
part of this is about departure

but its origin is a depression
and she will say
take any song you love

they all come from the same night
light toxics when it unfolds
all of us merry moon disappeared

but now at this time
let me forget the last tears
that flowed in my body

let me forget before it consumes
what remain of my life
clouds deeper upon the burning
mountain.

# Experiment of love where we once fall

i

and the water glitters
upon my body

as i glide on a meadow
i fall where sad faces
formed wall

music trumpet dance
in my heart i am building

a house with four windows
memory loss passion live

and its derogatory
a vowel etched on with pulses

of our yearnings
in my eyes a history can be so gripped

in my eyes two big shadows
hold each other, hand in hand

and become stitched by lamplight
when everyone burns candle

a voice creeps in with sound
of pimpernel. a cock learning

to keep water on its body
in my eyes there's a shadow disappearing

a part of ships excruciating
 in wilderness

ii

our ancestors say
the moon can reappear twice
in a day

only in the autumn
flowers pale with sea freezing

i sat to see my shadow
begging me leave

does love fall where light
cannot move through

it is light coming after love
our ancestors said

and it diminishes where love
is fractured

on my body
anyone can find a sea to swim

on my body i am building a house
where scars become doors

letting darkness escape
anyone can find where to enter

it is at the exit we all fall
for shadows. those still drowning.

# The decline of age

festos keeps old newspaper
in his bag
and travelled to kaduglei
to meet people ravaged by war
for many years
he keeps Sudan mirror
with headlines that speaks
of bombing of worship places
at night
how old the puzzle in the bottom
of paper, a puzzle of a man trying
to match all boxes with word of existence
here he sits to harbour moon in his palms
as it crosses fractures between the lines
and in his old days the headlines talk
about masses of people leaving home
for a single bullet
in front of him an old woman laid barefooted
tired of living in displacement camps
Festos can finish this puzzle only when his heart
is at peace, when Kaduglei is calm
and he's adamant some day in his newspaper
a man will get rid of existing with war, this black man.

# Jonathan

Jonathan, a fully grown man
still lies on the way to my door
wriggling his belt to become steady
in his conversation with god
he looked in the sky and foams
of smoke break into rainfall
too much easing away pieces
of blockage
that's bombing, that's negligence
how's home sleeping with people
desperate for rebirth
and when they are born today
they'll desert ways leading to oneness
is home this far
on my tongue tip
it's always catching fire, it can burn now
with the silence
and oh, the moon will rejuvenate life
from bounces of leaves
Jonathan lies still
as wind wrapped through his hair
and become an old balcony
keeping soft faces for remembrance.

# Take me to moseluem to touch on statue

today i passed through the fields
and a shadow runs after me
he says, "save the broken man"
give him milk if he's hungry
give him wine if he's thirsty
i wanted to save everything that walks
with him, arms heavy with life
hair scolded by fire and become
an epoch of a nice statue
living through air and thin
but he says his heroic ramblings can
keep me moving
after him a light shot on a windowpane
after him there's fire killing flies
eager to rest on his shadow
here i am running after him
not to fall victim of the blades gazumping
on tired bodies
after him i saw my grandmother knitting
beads on her waist
a way life never gives up when roads
are full of mud
after him i touched on the statue
to verify my identity
a member of burning candlelight.

# Burning city at night

on my wall dreams
stepped out like spiders
looking to enter into me
for revival

found cities burning
on my body

everyday sun become obscene
to appease a broken man

here i have shattered a mirror
to many pieces
to find real shape of my face

if at all it is broken
if it is a burning city at night

i will let everyone crave for fire
extinguishers to save my face

on my wall dreams
fit into tiny hole
and the mirror holds everything
for me

even shadows turning away from sunset.

# New voices in the rain

and i solely stepped into grass
to calm every burn on my body
everyday i find ways going home

and took to the street arranging
candles that separate midnight
from rest of the day

everyday i stand straight between
two glossy shadows
there is a new voice craving about

my restlessness to find where i can
live, it's not at home or across borders
people that remember how their feet

retraced in the book of history
the nature of their parental care
today sit to be counted among needful

and every drop of rain tells me
under my feet home gives you
anything desirable, living and existence
 it gives you where to belong.

# The height of moonlight

and he became incandescent
at the upfront
climbing hills with pure testimony
more decibels
more cries
at night he washes his fingers in a floral
pool
black stars parading
softly at the hemisphere
and see even on his fingers are homes
painted with reservoirs of life
green, grey and red
leaking often when too much light rises
on boabab trees
tonight he will say hallelujah
to reach the height of moonlight
people that existed through ways of leaving
leaves their homes to search for unending
light
where it is in the eyes of God
he buttoned holes that keeps water surging
in his chest
and become consistent in letting air
spill through despairing bodies
man, how many bodies you carry into paths
of moonlight
and never become everlasting in seeking
forgiveness when their hearts strayed
he leaves now, he will only come home at night

to place his hands on bounces of moon
he will only come to testify
how constantly it  is burning, home.

# After the rain drops

i came out this night
after rain revitalizes soil from harmatan
wind
to look for hailstones
falling over my roof
under my feet some lights can be seen
growing to cover all body parts
lights that emancipated movements
inside my heart
here the leaves can make me not regret
living in the rain
because under my feet are foams
of life swept into mud soil by current
of water
and it is the body escaping ways of drowning
this night the lamplight will keep burning
as is the line in my palms
this night my body will keep burning
to make all around me look better.

# Ama

these words are grown in my heart
beautiful like moon rising
on boabab trees
blistering like grass springing
on sud wetlands
how do i compare you ama
should i compare you to the birds
of beautiful toic
or cypress grass letting air walk through
or luster of new garden
ama, i have seen life moving softly
in your eyes
when i hold your hands to live in you
if i am moving at night
i compare you to the stars
finding a lost boy way back home
and if i am the tree
you are the leaves bringing shades to broken
birds
now, when i say all these, it is a broken boy
waiting for another embrace
drop the tears in your eyes, ama
and hear blasphemy in my heart
i am losing weight of the world
let me dance in the lights of your palms
i want to hold your hands, chin, breast
knowing i am always a free man to swim
on your body
if God is ever there to mend a torn heart
then you are the God that made me upright

for i am a man standing like a shattered
palace
once a beautiful place to live in
i will search for you like someone who's
tortoise had run into water
he hopes it will be found at last
ama, will i find you
to live for eternity
ama, will i find you to lift the decadent in my heart
i am eager for us to leave.

## some years late on

and then he poured water on a mud soil
mixed it with all ingredients soluble

and he said let there be light
and you rose gently among thousand stars

baba clapped his hands for hearing
i was searching for question of my living

how did the only man accorded all privileges
broke his faith

in the backyard he kissed a teenage girl
through barrel of a gun

and now his convulsions cannot be retracted
leave alone the wings that faded into unforeseeable
mirage

he said let there be water
and it is your body filling into lakes and rivers

can you find good measure for returning
your former self

everyone lost can ask where he left
you must know or someone will tell you

how to live
only now

## When the light cast on a dim altar

you'll know that man is not only made
from mud
but from light lost in the water
see, behind the tunnel a dog bark out
its anger
who knows the things in darkness
keep body still
one of them is to hold the rope
in your hands and hang yourself
last night in one of the prison
centers
a man torn his shirt trying to kill himself
who said men who took their lives
are afraid to live
i saw dogs refusing to carry fire
on their tales
they wanted to live as well
and started waving them to let us know
anything that keeps sadness in its eyes
can become happy when it learns
to let go of grievances
i am afraid, if the stars can move
why is this wall not luscious?
only the body made from water will not

break
now it will not drown
but will always be a river pulsating water
on stones
tonight it is full of people hiding their tears
of belonging
it is this night i realized thousand men
are afraid to live
 but not these ones who took their lives
alone
some of them lack good lamps to burn
whatever made darkness persistent
are you afraid, you live out of things with light
the altar keeping dim passages.

# The pathway

you have to step out with streak of light
pale eyes
and in your body a cobweb made ways
for the man despairing to reach
home
this is home like the stalk of long flower
doused by rainfall
you have made ways out of yourself
and how are the paths to enter
inside my body  to rekindle lost light
thus far beyond man's eyes
i saw few ones after the others stepping
out of trouble on my face
i saw scar closing like moon leaving into clouds
how many will miss its luscious burning.

# Body as a shipwreck for water

here in the middle of water
the sea can collect remainant of bodies
searching for belonging
and bring them where lights move
in the direction of music
playing songs like "we're going to lands
of longing birds"
here in the middle of water
the sun walk to retain its shadow
how's body not a shipwreck for water
and when night comes we all can revisit
the devastation of our footprints
swept away by hot humid wind
while we can lead ways for the playing birds
my father said
this is survival
this is history
can these birds learn songs once lasting
in their throats
or have they longed for fight
god, i am still asking for forgiveness
for keeping too much this silence.

# The first creation of loss

the first creation of loss
started when bird sit on lightbulb
looking into colour of its wings
today my father gives me gun
and think i am free to walk home alone
thousand fireflies breaking grass
with their lean bodies
find places they can rest awhile
five years ago
memories drop into liquidation
for leaving birds
those carrying homes on their feathers
can now resettle, can take their old footsteps
and reach the origin of creation
where humans live are creatures
flying beyond their boundaries
my father looked into his palms
and saw sun fragmented to tiny
lineage
those from broken glass
if you care about people hiding memories
in their eyes
there's loss keeping years fractured
and there's you folded behind any song
late in its composition

time will run out before you create
a redemption
my father says
you must have any sharp object boy
to become free
and i laced my tongue
not ready now for silences.

# After midnight song

till it becomes a song the body is calmed
maybe the world is loose
for fighting itself into a despairing man
and now is a notion exerted on the face

are you happy?

she says

the world is a midnight bird
its voice is  not owned.

## Boy, how do you live with a joy

bring me a black chair
pins and cobblestones under its wrecked
legs
bring me an umbrella
cloaked in dust to rewash it and dry
bring me an amber with lamps
soaked in paraffin
bring me tangles to swipe foams in the sky
and wet flowers bouqueted in red garden
bring me glimmers of new sunshine
brewing our feet to reset the destiny
bring me rainfall to moisten my heart
but,
do you have a belief
that good things may come your way
bring me joy
to washed off every pain brushed
on my chest
bring me fire
i want to burn that pride keeping me
burdened
bring me all you possess
i was born when leaves caught soreness
can they breathe, can they prattle
bring me water
i want to hide rivers in my palms
on my skin, you will not drown
you will only swim

and reach the shore
you will have all that belongs to you
the chair, fire and lamp
to light up your heart
and find a room flaked by joy
it is in you, just the touch in your heart
will you find a way to live.

# One night wiping mud faces

i forgot to walk into darkness
with knife tightened
between my fingers
pushing it at random
until it fell on a wall
cracked by rain

i forgot to hold its handle with all strength
in the palms

there are shadows
of people running away from severity of the night
falling on sharp edges
 split and run into blood

father said
to be free
i must have a gun

on my pillow
16 bullets sink in the eyes
dividing dreams with days of making one body
a shooting range

one eye blanked
and fire bullets on the chest of that mannequin

one eye blanked

and fire bullets on my head
to be cool

maybe it is calmness this way
to forgive our shadows leaving into
 graves
as an escape route

that night father said
i must have a gun to assume freedom
i held it on my chest
and counted souls dangling on the trigger
begging me to unplug

as others were seen moving in voluntarily
a way to be calm
and free.

# Four girls each smile alone

i

(1st girl)

she undressed
the wound
on her left leg

first

  flies compromised

second

 salt
melt on her toes

third

wind opens
wide

too many faces
scowl in the scar
captive expecting
to run out

how they went there?

her mother shot
in the stomach
refusing to give
her daughter to people
wallowed in flight wars

she took the bandage

tied
the wound

how it looks?

an enclave of graves
falling

the longer it remains
uncloaked

the longer pains
tickled her body.


ii

(2nd girl)


she took long
 rope
hanging between

two pillars
in a sturdy house

 petrol on a jar
burned windowsill

 first day

she saw herself
clipped on pale
mirror

she was smiling

 second day

she came to extinguish
fire burning all doors

 third day

she slept on clicking bed
the man she knows
a mountain
crashing on her body


iii

(3rd girl)


she was seated

on a cement
stool in the hospital

at 17 years

she gave birth to dead
twins

she's muddled
by damp blood
swept into sun

at 21 years

her friend
is a physiologist
in nearby p. h. c .u
examining bodies
on black table
to know ruptures
of birth operations

at 26 years

she and the husband
went to court
to be healed
from unsettled grips

how long will tears
bring her dead babies
to play under
the surpasses

of an escaping moon?

at 30 years


in a church next door
every star
rising she sees
her body falling
with the rain.


iv

(4th girl)


she holds
microphone
on a stage
with palisade of dim lights

she holds microphone
like the gun
jerked between earth and your jaws
wanting you
forgive her

she knows her mother
is innocent

she knows the debt her father acquired
was to built a concrete

home
with persistent roof

she knows smiling each alone
at night is to keep
men away

men tempted to fly into her body
with mouth of a gun

she is every story
spanning to next pages.

## Tonight if you sit among the culprits

you will know
the body destroyed
is the temple of God
you will stand up
looked at your watch
and saw seconds
ticking on
like age revealed
by slight grin
on the face
you will ask God
for forgiveness
you forsake
yourself
crunching on a five
year old girl
and disposed
her body into 8 meter
latrine
you looked at the sealing a maggot
break the soft wood
to specks of decadence
and you thought of the day
that girl begged you
to consider your gentleness
how you gave them bread

how you crack jokes
of thin moon
rising for the first time in the west
not enough for all leaves
how you knew
her father that day
among seven
dead between kenyi and limbe
how you became
the path leading
to her father
and you will shed
tears for damaging
the body of God

sat giddied
on a red soil

and you will shed tears
for breaking vows
of creation
sat on a stone
wishing its
 the girl
you will ask her forgiveness
and she will nod
placated of how you misappropriated
her body.

# I hide behind the mirror

when it is cloudy
heaven carry feet
of rainbow

like us with sun
keeping our shadows

and would sit
to spot a boy
tiptoeing onto more
blank pages

until his body
become mate
for too much running

on this mirror
are people
jerking their faces
behind its transparency

all quiet at once

raising hands
to answer are there
good things
in the roots
of flowers

one man held
 vast pot
of coruscating
petals on his chest
to safeguard
his holiness

one man
blazes the flowers
and each shadow
fades
till the wood
blending this mirror
broke

and bended to see faces
merged on blank pages
after being scattered by silence.

## Mama Amai

your body
is a butterfly
carrying rain
on its wings

i feel touches
of moon
when my eyes
glued to watch
night leaving
behind stars

if i can hold
you like moses
with his rod
would throw
you upon a sparkling
aisle
more enkindled
on your cornrows

    you'll be the sea
swooping my body
ashore

"and me a fish
that swallowed

jona"

here in a pulling
tide
i am lounging to scarper
vanishes of descending
sun

inside my palms
i have always
seen faces
sowed by love

and you were
a raving citadel
worshiped
by kings
when they are constantly
dithered by wreckages

some of us
were unjustified
to bury your heart

for loving

for faith

for truthfulness

your body is a butterfly
carrying rain
on its wings

Mama Amai
is beauty molded
from pain?

# Night later

i wished for lips
longing for the night,
when prettier things
become a surgical
blade
my life holds every
question
from that night mother
leaves me to buzzing
of mosquitoes,
i kept myself awake
to give testimonies
of maceration,
to give my body one last kiss
and scratch it with these grown nails.
these scars are mirrors to rekindle a memory
but tonight any sigh is a grief
taking us into forgetfulness.
that night mother said
the way for a broken
man is struggle,
i was a boy trying to hide love in my eyes.
that night mother walked into dim streets
to recover what is lost in me,
to energize, to manufacture.
i knew it was love,
 she wept for the question dashed on my tongue,
of how to survive the rain?
that night mother walked into my room

and burn the candle dead before midnight,
she searched for life on my face
but i was filled with dreams of 12 years
that was the credo, the joy, the leaving
and knew what was burnt in me is a living.
that night mother gave me her wings
and i flew away from this tempting night
to a crossable river.

# A little toy city

at the tip of toy city
parades thousand cadres
with helmets prehistoric to their coming
the house stand on the bank
of the only river holding salt as water
that river fogged by morning wetness
presumes its elevation, becomes erotic
to fondling of rain
reverberating and wailing and resurfacing
and secreting feet like sculptures cut on clay
soil
and recuperate their second coming
in so much time everything becomes myth
and the river respond to the grunting
of sky
and flake to more dry places
and circle the mountain and it soggy
channels become soggier and cuddled
to embrace bodies yearning to wash
smashes out, bodies unbridled by mud
this is how a little toy city was erected
to keep cadres into sensation
with their war days, all fighting incapacitation
all now incapable of enjoying their production
and as the rain swiftly sojourned
the river moved back ward
robbed of its sensual mimicry
and the little city held people
to its outmost center and set them out

later when love is a pride.

## A sad night to love eliza

one evening eliza
waded to bosky
dent of fireflies,
a stench flew into her nose
after residue of earth
awaken to life
by the rain.
in the midst of lambent stars
her friend sat and clapped at all biting creatures,
shifting greenwards
after dew drenched
his shirt,
a touch of warmth on his chest,
so malleable,
elusive of million kisses.
even in two life is formidable to the nature,
a moon slides always retracing our lineage
and when they gaze in the shades of palmtrees
a hand reached from beyond
mending two to one.
it was night later eliza strolled to nearby bistros
and found his friend lying on a broken chair,
she whispered to him how often some flex feelings
may impede living
but the sky shuddered its lights
and wrote,

"these are my children i adore so much".
she felt on his chest
and became candlesticks tinkered by fire.
left to solitude as bodies
run to compassionate separation.
panicking.
*that night eliza left with broken lamp into dark room.*

# Night i crave for your soul

i'll wait for you kush
inside wild forests and severe grasses
my hands will stretch for you
for the touch of your fingers sweet love
till your heart reconcile with mine
i'll absorb domestic flowers for you
love
hiding beneath din of palm trees
keeping all belongings to yourself
i am bound to take your hand
and move back home
 as broken lovers
and sit on this balcony like strangers
waiting for their sentences
like flowers woken by night's feet
my heart cut long in absence
let me hold onto you forever
sweet love
and do not say i am a fool to follow
all directions your shadow moves.

# The second rash to kush love

i'll sit here kush
like a child waiting for his departed mother
staring at the fall of every dry leaf
i shall break my silence with terrific sputters of white nile
i shall amuse myself with touches on shambe's spring
night dread over my molluscum skin
yet i saw myself falling apart
torn from perpetual glue that bounded us together
oh sweet kush!
love is beautiful,
it merges one's soul to darkness
and finds infinite light in it
i shall inhale such life on this bank
and watch you sweet love springing
beneath soft cypresses
kush,
i stood here staring at the rays of the sun
yet tears fall on my toes
i am afraid my heart is broken
come hold me tight
my soul has taken ways
could it be that you are another dimension
sweet kush,
let's fill nile with silent kisses
*we're never more separable.*

## At 11:36 am

and when sun rises and rises
and rises and rises again
it is always the same with that one
standing alone yesterday
you can see it animated
on a glossy paper
stretching its feet to last margins
and glimpses back a thousand times to shine
you can see it tanning my fingers
overheating those which are low
under my shadow
even with much water sopping
there is that one forcing itself
to be closer to me
you can see it flouting my hair
becoming passable by many winds
and when that sun rises
and rises again
it becomes much relentless than the one
of yesterday
and i become too hard to crevice now
this is because i did not realize
every rising sun has been a force
nudging me on
you can see it blended
on a slummed window
longing for a more permanent home
that one not giving up to catastrophes
and reconsider hands tickling it to forget
of a guilt once carried to sediments

you can see it dip on my body
unleashing its roots
to pores capable of ferrying air into my skin
and grow trees with shafts
keeping smaller ones like needles
to suppress those aiming to climb
this is only complete
when a life is spotted in our sad eyes
and when sun rises
and rises again
it spreads on all perches led by that wind
this is because i did not know i am wider now
too vast to be tethered
maybe when it ditches windows
i will dispose myself to much tinnier folders
unable to be handled by deceptive fingers
this is because the sun rises
and rises and rises again.

# More at a constant road

more at a constant
road

a flaring petal
envisage

this man
plunging
into sack of sorghum

more at a constant
feud
of heart

a droplet
of rain tarnishes
radiant fleshing
of grain

the eye can see
what heart cannot conceive

the nose smell
what mouth cannot
swallow

2 mountains
each a bizarre
gauze field

2 graveyards
descending one
after another

this man seeking
happen days

more at a constant
starvation

the feet can walk
what hands cannot
hold onto.

## The russet home

and its fields are white as hailstones
      in the rain
the lambent gape of petals
      leaning towards mud wall
consumes beauty spread
      in the sky
and the fields are easily barren
      when the sun dipped on its orbs
here is a house keeping men
      eagerly awaiting moonlight over sun
at last the lights stupor man's ambitions
      of running into thunderbolt
    come on dudes, are you not tired
of sinking into wet desires
      all are broken, all are your soft tears
hidden in the palms
and are as white as rain itself
      the swiftest way to break rain water
is to let it fall on a dry earth
      you will have caught its smell from the window
and know inside here
      some men got paranoid for trying to be everlasting fire.

**The leaving**

## (After Alphonso Cikedi)

and it was this far
he walked into the wood
just to know his world
is gripped by indefinable power
and cited to go back home
to find his unwitting feet all intrusive
through these contours of life
he resembles a guard
in the ancient times of gilgamesh
and his work emulated gilgamesh
himself, thirsty of many journeys
 his followers
would say, take this route
sometimes everyone will point
a way for him
and he will say, he knows where's heading
he knows and will not come back
maybe that is how to let go of pasts
or to embroils oneself in mistakes
sometimes everyone will offer to help him
and he would say,
this is where i want to go.

# Antiquity of a night painting

### (1)

tonight i want to dare this prayer     to exist to see through my
palms  images of father reaching out for despairing child
  now am i that child     jumping into water assuring his
cleanliness
am i that hopeful    waiting for sun to caress clouds   for
tomorrow's moisture  for us to be one we looked at each other's
palms       drawn the same
now i am that diverse tribe    randomized on the maps  cleavaging
themselves for survival
God, give me this profound
burning fire to be quiet.

# Her question of life

night before her lover comes
home
she undressed her body into pools
of night rain
forming bathtub in a back room
and the lover jumped on her body
like white bird on a grazing sheep
like butterfly in a wet land
where all inhaled is softness of rain on grass
and she said
come on, let's breathe stars and moons
and light walked onto her thighs
and the lover knelt as it becomes stern
to keep feet of all that shines
that time she placed hands on his face
and felt warmth of her loving heart
on the ribs
man is made from dust and looked
into sun for more running
and saw life foamed under his feet
more than the eyes
is man ever free to walk back into water
and become the pools of rain
falling on night roofs
she took her palms and cut tiny
lines
for fire to burn all days
and her lover desired more intensity
like rain forming bathtub

that time they knew how to run away
from death by kissing palms
and live softly wearing night
into good love
man, is there life in the aftermath of lights?

# Love or affluence, girl

girl

a. our boys
do not want to talk
they hide bullets in their mouths

b. kiss the hell out of them
and sink into pit of sulphur

c. girl
what have you got to live for

d. love or affluence?

## In our old days

we loved to talk of revolutionaries
like john garang, karbino kuanyin,
brainstorming of unexplained powers of manyang jok
and the unforgiving power of tong luoc –
about how he could dance in fire
without burning his skin.

the moon was always bright yet we could be blind in plays,
plays like to go and hide under the crops,
plays like to tie your face and blindly chose your girlfriend,
we still remember those days when we sit here in camps,
when we run to queue to be given free grain
again.

my grandfather always swore when he saw fish packed
that i would never eat that which my hands never cut open.
when a bullet would be left to your house
and our night playing girls gathered to prepare food for the
revolutionaries.

sweet tears dripped down our cheeks
although it was said to generations to never think of the past,
how could our minds let them be bygones
when we could leave homes for weed and moss.
ah, now lonhmagok roamed like a rejected harlot among enemies,
if i could be snow to come and fade later in the day
i could come and glance on my old days,
 calmly on a giant rock.

# My life

my life
a little drop in the ocean
searching for its end
i found dry leaves deep
underground
and say
a fisher man was once a dry leaf
swung into the sea
by winds
but most days i am a rain
mending crevices on the land
i swear life can only grow
when one turns over
a new leaf
hopes are figment on these leaves
letting air fills them with life
even when wind stop
moving the grass
would still dance
it cannot change directions
but times keep me
stand by the window
seeing seasons unfolding
and say
life has got fingers to tickle
a soul unwilling to fly with butterflies.

## do not sleep child

do not sleep child
take this pen and write down your name
it will always remain this earth the same
they are running to fight
but down here I am giving you light
be always happy to learn every day
it's not a shame to boycott politics
keep feeding your mind
and you will always live to be kind
do not sleep child
tomorrow morning you must live well
rewriting days they wished you farewell
how many cows will you buy in a day
for your elder brother sent you on a mission
while you live discourage these divisions
to know world around you
will never make you stranger in your own land
do not sleep child
in you
the community will stand
do not sleep this is the day
to find for them brighter way
giving them what they had to pay
do not sleep child.

## Mmap New African Poets Series

If you have enjoyed *Broken Maps*, consider these other fine books in the **Mmap New African Poets Series** from *Mwanaka Media and Publishing*:

*I Threw a Star in a Wine Glass* by Fethi Sassi
*Best New African Poets 2017 Anthology* by Tendai R Mwanaka and Daniel Da Purificacao
*Logbook Written by a Drifter* by Tendai Rinos Mwanaka
*Mad Bob Republic: Bloodlines, Bile and a Crying Child* by Tendai Rinos Mwanaka
*Zimbolicious Poetry Vol 1* by Tendai R Mwanaka and Edward Dzonze
*Zimbolicious Poetry Vol 2* by Tendai R Mwanaka and Edward Dzonze
*Zimbolicious: An Anthology of Zimbabwean Literature and Arts, Vol 3* by Tendai Mwanaka
*Under The Steel Yoke* by Jabulani Mzinyathi
*Fly in a Beehive* by Thato Tshukudu
*Bounding for Light* by Richard Mbuthia
*Sentiments* by Jackson Matimba
*Best New African Poets 2018 Anthology* by Tendai R Mwanaka and Nsah Mala
*Words That Matter* by Gerry Sikazwe
*The Ungendered* by Delia Watterson
*Ghetto Symphony* by Mandla Mavolwane
*Sky for a Foreign Bird* by Fethi Sassi
*A Portrait of Defiance* by Tendai Rinos Mwanaka
*Zimbolicious: An Anthology of Zimbabwean Literature and Arts, Vol 4* by Tendai Mwanaka and Jabulani Mzinyathi
*When Escape Becomes the only Lover* by Tendai R Mwanaka
*وَيَسْ هَرُ اللَّيْلُ فِى شَفَتَي...وَلِعَمَام* by Fethi Sassi
*A Letter to the President* by Mbizo Chirasha
*This is not a poem* by Richard Inya

*Pressed flowers* by John Eppel
*Righteous Indignation* by Jabulani Mzinyathi:
*Blooming Cactus* by Mikateko Mbambo
*Rhythm of Life* by Olivia Ngozi Osouha
*Travellers Gather Dust and Lust* by Gabriel Awuah Mainoo
*Chitungwiza Mushamukuru: An Anthology from Zimbabwe's Biggest Ghetto Town* by Tendai Rinos Mwanaka
*Zimbolicious: An Anthology of Zimbabwean Literature and Arts, Vol 5* by Tendai Mwanaka
*Because Sadness is Beautiful?* by Tanaka Chidora
*Of Fresh Bloom and Smoke* by Abigail George
*Shades of Black* by Edward Dzonze
*Best New African Poets 2020 Anthology* by Tendai Rinos Mwanaka, Lorna Telma Zita and Balddine Moussa
*This Body is an Empty Vessel* by Beaton Galafa
*Between Places* by Tendai Rinos Mwanaka
*Best New African Poets 2021 Anthology* by Tendai Rinos Mwanaka, Lorna Telma Zita and Balddine Moussa
*Zimbolicious: An Anthology of Zimbabwean Literature and Arts, Vol 6* by Tendai Mwanaka and Chenjerai Mhondera
*A Matter of Inclusion* by Chad Norman
*Keeping the Sun Secret* by Mariel Awendit
*ہەلتەلّبوتّٹ جلّ سر*by Tendai Rinos Mwanaka
*Ghetto Blues* by Tendai Rinos Mwanaka
*Zimbolicious: An Anthology of Zimbabwean Literature and Arts, Vol 7* by Tendai Rinos Mwanaka and Tanaka Chidora
*Best New African Poets 2022 Anthology* by Tendai Rinos Mwanaka and Helder Simbad
*Dark Lines of History* by Sithembele Isaac Xhegwana
*a sky is falling* by Nica Cornell
*Death of a Statue* by Samuel Chuma
*Along the way* by Jabulani Mzinyathi
*Strides of Hope* by Tawanda Chigavazira

*Young Galaxies* by Abigail George
*Coming of Age* by Gift Sakirai
*Mother's Kitchen and Other Places* by *Antreka. M. Tladi*
*Best New African Poets 2023 Anthology* by Tendai Rinos Mwanaka, Helder Simbad and Gerald Mpesse
*Zimbolicious Anthology Vol 8* by Tendai Rinos Mwanaka and Mathew T Chikono

**Soon to be released**
*Formless by* Raïs Neza Boneza
*Of poets, gods, ghosts. Irritants and storytellers* by Tendai Rinos Mwanaka

www.ingramcontent.com/pod-product-compliance
Lightning Source LLC
Chambersburg PA
CBHW070939180426
43192CB00039B/2339